My Hindu Year

Cath Senker

Titles in this series
My Buddhist Year • My Christian Year • My Hindu Year
My Jewish Year • My Muslim Year • My Sikh Year

Conceived and produced for Hodder Wayland by

Nutshell
MEDIA

Intergen House, 65-67 Western Road, Hove, BN3 2JQ, UK
www.nutshellmedialtd.co.uk

Editor: Polly Goodman
Inside designer and illustrator: Peta Morey
Cover designer: Tim Mayer
Consultant: Rasamandala Das, ISKCON Educational Services

Published in Great Britain in 2003 by Hodder Wayland, an imprint of Hodder Children's Books.

This paperback edition published in 2004

The website addresses (URLs) included in this book were valid at the time of going to press. However, because of the nature of the Internet, it is possible that some addresses may have changed, or sites may have changed or closed down since publication. While the author and Publisher regret any inconvenience this may cause readers, no responsibility for any such changes can be accepted by either the author or the Publisher.

British Library Cataloguing in Publication Data
Senker, Cath
My Hindu year. - (A year of religious festivals)
1. Fasts and feasts - Hinduism - Juvenile literature
I. Title
294.5'36

ISBN 0 7502 4057 1

Printed in China

Hodder Children's Books
A division of Hodder Headline Limited
338 Euston Road, London NW1 3BH

Acknowledgements: The author would like to thank Dhara, Lata, Bhupendra and Darshan Patel for all their help in the preparation of this book.

Picture Acknowledgements:
Art Directors & Trip Photo Library 13 (R. Belbin), 16 (Eric Smith), 17 (Resource Foto), 21, 23, 24 (H. Rogers); Britstock 4 (Hideo Haga); Chapel Studios 20 (B. Mistry); Circa Photo Library Cover, 6 (John Smith), 7 (William Holtby), 8, 15, 27 (John Smith); Impact Photos Title page (Robin Laurence), 10 (J. L. Dugast), 14 (M. de Vries); Nutshell Media 5 (Yiorgos Nikiteas); World Religions 9 (C. Stout), 11, 12, 18 (P. Kapoor), 19, 22 (Christine Osborne), 25 (C. Stout), 26 (Nick Dawson).

Cover photograph: Having fun with paint and coloured water at the Holi festival.
Title page: Children with painted faces for Holi.

Contents

A Hindu life

Hindus believe there is one God. He is everywhere. God is always loving, but he can also get angry.

Hindus have many beliefs about God, the world and the people in it. They see God in many forms, as gods and goddesses. Many Hindu festivals are about these gods and goddesses.

Images of Hindu gods in a temple, from left to right: Ganesha, Lakshmi, Durga and Saraswati.

This is Dhara. She has written a diary about the Hindu festivals.

Dhara's diary
Saturday 11 October

My name's Dhara Patel. I'm eight years old. I've got a brother called Darshan, who's twelve. We live with our mum, dad and grandmother. My dad's from Gujarat in India and my mum's from Uganda, and before that Gujarat. My family is Hindu. At home we always eat vegetarian food. I like dancing, painting, and playing with my friends. My favourite festival is Navaratri.

Hindus have lots of holy books, such as the *Vedas*. They teach people how to worship God.

The Hindu symbol is called Aum.

Daily worship

Every day

Hindus worship every day at home. Worship is called puja. Hindus have a shrine in their homes where they do puja.

At the shrine, Hindus make offerings to a murti. A murti is a sacred statue of God, or a god or goddess.

This girl is making an offering to an image of Krishna.

Hindus in India gathering at the mandir for worship.

Hindus also go to the mandir (temple) to worship. Outside India, people mainly gather at the mandir at the weekend.

Dhara's diary
Saturday 18 October

Today we went to the mandir. We sat down and prayed to God. Afterwards we sang songs. We always go to the mandir to celebrate the festivals. The best thing about going there is eating delicious food! We also have a shrine at home where we worship every day. There are murtis of the gods Ganesha and Krishna, and the goddess Saraswati.

Divali

October/November

Divali is a joyful festival of lights. It celebrates the return of Rama and Sita, in the story from the *Ramayana*.

The story shows how good wins over evil. People light divas (oil lamps) to welcome Rama and Sita.

This family has lit diva lamps in front of their shrine for Divali.

Rangoli patterns are often made in swirls or the shape of flowers.

Sunday 26 October

Yesterday was Divali. We had lights everywhere. I wore my *chaniya choli*, a beautiful dress I only wear on special occasions. We said 'Happy Divali' to everyone. I entered a rangoli competition but I didn't win. I got a trophy for dancing though. We went to the mandir and prayed for a good year. We shared sweets. Later, at home, we made poppadoms. Delicious!

At Divali, people make rangoli patterns from coloured rice powder. They hope the goddess Lakshmi will see the beautiful patterns and visit their homes. Hindus pray to Lakshmi to bring them good luck in the coming year.

Saraswati Puja

January/February

This festival celebrates the goddess Saraswati and the first day of spring. Saraswati is the goddess of learning. She is also the goddess of music, poetry, dance and drama.

People wear bright yellow clothes at this festival. Yellow stands for the warmth of spring.

The beautiful goddess Saraswati is shown playing an instrument called a vina.

Children playing traditional Indian instruments. The girl is playing the harmonium. The boy is playing the tablas.

Dhara's diary
Monday 29 January

Today it was Saraswati Puja. We didn't do anything special for this festival except pray to the goddess Saraswati for blessings. We prayed that when we grow up, we won't have many problems. Saraswati's favourite instrument is the vina, which is played a bit like a guitar. She plays classical Indian music.

In Bengal, people carry giant images of Saraswati around the streets. At the end of the day, they say goodbye to the images by placing them in the river. Music is played for all to enjoy.

Mahashivaratri

February/March

The name of this festival means the 'Great Night of Shiva'. It celebrates Shiva, one of the most important forms of God.

Mahashivaratri is a solemn festival. Some Hindu families fast. At the mandir, people pour milk over a stone column called the Shiva Linga. This is to honour Shiva.

A boy in India washing a Shiva Linga with milk.

A woman dancing a popular Indian dance for Mahashivaratri.

Shiva is also known as the 'Lord of the Dance'. Hindus believe he dances a special dance on Mahashivaratri.

Dhara's diary
Thursday 19 February

Yesterday was Mahashivaratri, Shiva's birthday. When Shiva dances, sometimes he shows his anger and sometimes his happiness. It was a fast day, which means we only ate certain foods. We fasted to clean our bodies. I helped to make sago patties, which are small white pies. We ate them with sweet potatoes. They were yummy. We didn't eat sugar, rice or green vegetables. We broke our fast in the evening.

Holi

February/March

Holi is a joyful festival at springtime. There are bonfires, processions, music and dancing.

Hindus remember the story of Lord Krishna, a form of God. When he was young, Krishna loved to play tricks and have fun. Krishna, his friends and his relatives used to throw coloured water over each other.

People in West Bengal, India, enjoying a water fight with coloured water at Holi.

This boy in Britain is having fun spraying his friends with coloured powder around the Holi bonfire.

At Holi people celebrate the love between Krishna and all living things. Children go out into the streets and splash each other with brightly coloured water.

Dhara's diary
Sunday 7 March

Yesterday it was Holi. We went to the mandir wearing white clothes and threw coloured water all over each other. We got completely covered in it! My friends played tricks, too, like hiding from each other. We did this to remember how Krishna loved playing tricks when he was young. Then we ate long noodles, boiled with sugar and ghee.

Ramnavami

March/April

Ramnavami is a happy festival. It celebrates the birthday of Rama, a form of God. He came down to Earth to stop evil in the world.

Rama is the hero of the famous story, the *Ramayana*. His faithful servant was Hanuman, the monkey king. Hanuman helped to rescue Rama's wife, Sita.

The *Ramayana* story being acted out in Indonesia. It is a very long performance.

This couple in India are dressed up as Rama (left) and Sita (right). They are the main people in the *Ramayana* story.

Dhara's diary
Thursday 1 April

On Tuesday it was Rama's birthday. We dressed in our best clothes and went to the mandir. We bathed the murti of Rama in water and milk. Then we sang songs. Some people went to the mandir every day for seven days but we just went once. I like the stories from the *Ramayana*. My favourite person is Sita.

At Ramnavami, people read or act out parts of the *Ramayana*. At the mandir, a murti of baby Rama is placed in a cradle.

Ratha Yatra

June/July

Ratha Yatra is a grand festival in India and England. In some places, thousands of Hindus join in.

Ratha Yatra means 'the journey of the chariot'. In Puri, east India, people pull three huge chariots through their town. There is a murti on each chariot.

Here in Puri, east India, the chariots have stopped to let people see the murtis.

The Ratha Yatra chariot at a procession in Britain. When Ratha Yatra is celebrated in Britain, there is usually just one chariot.

The murtis on the chariots are Jagannath, his brother and his sister. Jagannath is another name for Krishna. People tell stories about him and sing songs.

Dhara's diary
Saturday 19 June

Today it was Ratha Yatra. A small procession went round a few streets near our home. Everyone gathered in their best clothes and there was dancing. Then everyone went home to cook some tasty food. In India, the roads are closed for the day of Ratha Yatra because the processions are so big. I'd love to go to Ratha Yatra in India one day.

Raksha Bandhan

July/August

At Raksha Bandhan, brothers and sisters show their love for each other. Every sister marks her brother's forehead with a special paste. Then she puts rice grains on the mark.

She ties a rakhi around her brother's wrist. A rakhi is a bracelet made from thread. It is to protect him from evil.

This girl is tying a rakhi around her brother's wrist.

This brother and sister are giving each other delicious Indian sweets at Raksha Bandhan.

Dhara's diary

Sunday 31 August

Yesterday it was Raksha Bandhan. I made a rakhi for my brother Darshan and tied it on to his wrist. I gave him a blessing and he gave me some money. I felt proud of my brother yesterday. I also sent rakhis to my cousins Kunj and Kevin in Canada. When they come to visit, they'll give me a present.

The sister puts a sweet called barfi in her brother's mouth. He gives her a present and promises to look after her.

Krishna Janmashtami

August/September

This happy festival celebrates Krishna's birth. For some Hindus, this is the most important festival.

Hindus believe that Krishna was born at midnight. In the evening, they meet at the mandir. They move lamps in circles in front of the murtis. This is the arti ceremony.

These children are helping to perform the arti ceremony.

Baby Krishna (left) and his brother Balaram stealing buttermilk. It is said that Krishna loved milky foods.

People sing religious songs about Krishna, called bhajans. There is dancing too. Many Hindus fast all day until midnight. At midnight, they share fruit and sweets, or a big meal.

Dhara's diary
Tuesday 7 September

Last night it was Krishna's birthday. We went to the mandir and sang songs. There was a cradle holding a murti of baby Krishna. At midnight, bells were rung to celebrate Krishna's birth. We took it in turns to rock the cradle. By then we were really hungry. We ate a proper meal at the mandir, with puris, rice and dhal. It was delicious!

Ganesha Chaturthi

August/September

Ganesha is a popular god. He has an elephant's head. Many Hindu families have a murti of him at home.

For this festival, in western India, people make clay images of Ganesha. They place them in their home shrines. At morning and evening prayers they pray to Ganesha.

An image of Ganesha, the god of wisdom, good luck and riches.

An image of Ganesha is carried down to the lake in Gujarat, India.

Saturday 18 September

Today we celebrated Ganesha Chaturthi at the mandir. We prayed to Ganesha and then to the other gods. We sat down and a group of people sang songs. Then we sang them too. Afterwards, we ate a shared meal. Some people stayed in the mandir to pray again. We always pray to Ganesha at home. I pray to him if I'm worried about something.

Everyone enjoys singing bhajans, especially children. At the end of the festival, huge crowds carry the images of Ganesha to the sea, river or lake. They plunge them into the water.

Navaratri

September/October

Navaratri means 'nine nights'. At this lively festival, Hindus worship different mother goddesses.

The main goddess is Lord Shiva's wife. She is often called Parvati or Durga.

At the end of the festival, these Hindus in Bangladesh place an image of Durga in the river to say goodbye.

People dancing the stick dance, called *dandya ras,* **at Navaratri.**

Everyone dances around a special shrine. It has pictures of the mother goddesses on it. There are two special dances, a circle dance and a stick dance.

Hindus of all ages dance and sing into the night. Some people join in every evening for nine days!

Dhara's diary
Saturday 23 October

Navaratri is really good fun. Last night we went to the hall to dance. We made a circle with the goddesses in the middle and danced around them. Then some people sang, and others clapped. Next we did arti, and after that we did the stick dance. I was exhausted! Before we went home we ate a good meal.

Festival calendar

October/November
Divali
The festival of lights.

January
Lohri
A one-day festival to celebrate the end of the winter season, celebrated mainly in Punjab, northern India. Bonfires are lit.

January
Pongal
A three-day festival in southern India that starts on exactly the same day as Lohri. It celebrates the rice harvest. Rice boiled in milk is offered to the sun-god, Surya.

January/February
Saraswati Puja
A spring festival to worship Saraswati, the goddess of learning.

February/March
Mahashivaratri
The main festival to worship Shiva.

February/March
Holi
A spring festival. People spray each other with coloured water and make bonfires.

March/April
Ramnavami
This festival celebrates Rama's birthday.

June/July
Ratha Yatra
A festival to worship Krishna. Huge chariots with images of Krishna, his brother and his sister are pulled through the streets.

July/August
Raksha Bandhan
A special festival for brothers and sisters.

August/September
Krishna Janmashtami
The celebration of Lord Krishna's birthday.

August/September
Ganesha Chaturthi
The main festival for the worship of Ganesha.

September/October
Navaratri and Durgapuja
Celebrations of the mother goddess.

September/October
Dassehra
People act out the story of Rama's victory over the demon Ravana.

Glossary

arti Lighting candles and moving them in a circle. It is done in front of images of gods to honour them.

barfi A sweet made from milk and sugar.

bhajans Songs to glorify God. Musicians usually play along with the singers.

blessings God's help and protection.

diva A lamp made from twisted cotton wool dipped in melted butter. It is lit during worship. Many divas are lit at Divali.

Ganesha The god with an elephant head. He is kind to all living things.

ghee Oil made from melted butter.

Hanuman The monkey god.

honour To show that you admire and respect a person, or God.

Krishna One of the most popular forms of God, who came to Earth about 5,000 years ago.

Lakshmi The goddess of wealth.

mandir A place of worship for Hindus, sometimes called a temple.

murti This word means 'form'. It is the image or sacred statue of God, or a god or goddess, used in worship.

offerings Things that are offered to the image of a god, to ask for blessings.

puja Worship, at home or at the mandir. People usually worship at a shrine with images of gods and goddesses.

rakhi A bracelet, usually made from cotton or silk.

Rama The hero of the *Ramayana* story. He came to Earth as a form of God.

Ramayana One of the important Hindu holy books. It is a poem with 24,000 verses.

rangoli A beautiful pattern made at the entrance of homes and mandirs. The rangoli pattern is to welcome gods and visitors.

Saraswati The goddess of learning.

Sita Rama's wife.

Vedas Very old holy books that tell Hindus how to worship God.

Notes for teachers

pp4–5 Three main forms of God are Vishnu, Shiva and Shakti, who are the main focuses of worship. Hindu customs and festivals are very diverse. They vary depending on which part of India people live in or where their family comes from. Two forms of scriptures exist: the *shruti* (revealed truths) are scriptures that were revealed to holy men, including the *Vedas*; the *smiriti* (remembered truths) consist of religious literature such as the Hindu epics, the *Ramayana* and the *Mahabharata*. Dhara's family are vegetarian. Many Hindus are vegetarians because they don't want to harm animals.

pp6–7 Hindus hold differing views about God. Some believe that there is one God, and the other gods and goddesses are lesser deities. Others believe that all gods and goddesses are equal, and represent the various features of the one God. At the beginning or end of puja there will often be an arti ceremony, for showing reverence to a deity. An oil lamp is held by a worshipper and a circle of light made in front of an image of a god or goddess.

pp8–9 When Rama and Sita returned home after 14 years in exile, it was the night of the new moon, and extremely dark. Their route was lit with candles so that they could see the way. This is one of the reasons behind the lights at Divali. Divali is about new beginnings; people spring clean their homes and the mandir. It is the start of the new financial year, so people hope that Lakshmi will bless them with prosperity. Rangoli patterns are a way of welcoming visitors.

pp10–11 The goddess is an important form of God. Some describe her as Shakti, the energy of the universe. She takes a variety of forms, usually consorts of corresponding male deities. Shakti most specifically refers to Parvati, the consort of Shiva, and her forms such as Durga and Kati. Lakshmi, the goddess of wealth, is the wife of Vishnu. Saraswati, the goddess of learning, is the consort of Brahma, the creator. For certain festivals temporary deities are made, which are then immersed in water at the end of the celebrations as a respectful farewell gesture.

pp12–13 In the Hindu legends, Shiva is shown in many different forms. As Lord of the Dance, he is a symbol of the eternal energy that flows through the world. This energy causes day and night, the pattern of the seasons, and birth and death. Dhara refers to Shiva's anger because Shiva's dancing destroys the universe. The energy of his dance then recreates a new universe. This pattern is repeated throughout time.

pp14–15 At Holi two main stories are remembered: the story of Prahlada and the story of Lord Krishna and Princess Radha (Krishna's girlfriend). A bonfire is lit to remember Prahlada. King Hiranyakashipu was a materialistic and atheistic king, who hated the way his saintly son Prahlada worshipped Vishnu. He ordered that Prahlada be put on a bonfire, but Vishnu saved him. At Holi, Hindus celebrate good winning over evil. They bring offerings, including coconut, a symbol of new life, to throw on the bonfire.

pp16–17 An avatar is a form of God who comes to Earth to protect the pious, destroy the wicked and re-establish real religion. Rama is an avatar of Vishnu. Hindus believe that Vishnu has appeared on Earth in different forms nine times, to ensure that good defeats evil. They believe that Vishnu will come again in the future to destroy evil and create a new world. Ramnavani is a day of fasting. A murti of baby Rama is bathed to symbolically honour and worship him.

pp18–19 Many Hindus think of Krishna as Lord of the Universe, and Ratha Yatra is celebrated in grand style. In Puri, east India, the whole town is involved in the ceremony. Various religious rites take place before the procession, and as it moves forward, musicians play pipes and trumpets. At the original Ratha Yatra festival in Puri, there are three chariots, one for each murti, but in England there is usually only one. We get the word 'juggernaut' from Jagannath, the giant deity who is seated on a chariot.

pp20–21 'Raksha' means 'protection' and 'Bandhan' means 'to tie'. The purpose of Raksha Bandhan is to reaffirm family bonds. It is the dharma, or duty, of siblings to be caring towards each other. The festival is celebrated by people of all ages. If a girl does not have a brother, the ceremony can be carried out with cousins – she may send rakhis in the post, for example to relatives in India. The rakhi is usually made of cotton or silk, and is worn until it falls off.

pp22–23 During the day leading up to Krishna's birth, Hindus may fast, or just eat fruit and milk. In countries outside India, some Hindus celebrate Krishna's birth when it strikes midnight in India, for example, at 7.30 p.m. in England. Other rituals at this festival include ringing bells and blowing the conch shell to announce Krishna's birth. At this festival, many Hindus eat delicacies prepared from milk and butter because Krishna loved such foods.

pp24–25 Ganesha, son of Shiva and Parvati, has an elephant's head. According to one story, Shiva chopped off Ganesha's head in a fit of anger. Parvati demanded that Shiva restore Ganesha to life but Shiva couldn't find the head. He resolved to fit the head of the first living being he saw on to his son; the first creature he spotted was an elephant. In India, elephants are used to clear obstacles, such as tree trunks. People pray to Ganesha to remove problems that stand in their way. They pray to him before religious rituals or important events, such as exams.

pp26–27 Hindus believe that by partaking in this festival, they can awaken the mother goddess's energy and use it to defeat evil that is present in daily life. The festival has different names in different parts of India, and the celebrations vary. Navaratri is an important Gujarati festival, also popular in Britain. In Bengal, the goddess Durga is worshipped. The day after the nine nights of the festival, the images of Durga are immersed in a river. In northern India, the festival is called Dassehra, and is connected with the story of Rama defeating the demon Ravana.

p28 Hindus use a lunar calendar called the Panchang, which has 12 lunar months.

Other resources

Artefacts
Articles of Faith, Resource House, Kay Street, Bury, Lancashire BL9 6BU Tel. 0161 763 6232
Gohil Emporium (Religious Artefacts from India), 381 Stratford Road, Birmingham B11 4JZ Tel. 0121 771 3048.
ISKCON Educational Services, Bhaktivedanta Manor, Hilfield Lane, Aldenham, Watford, Herts WD2 8EZ Artefacts, resources and information. Tel. 01923 859578 Website: www.iskcon.org.uk

Religion in Evidence, 28b Nunnbrook Road Industrial Estate, Huthwaite, Nottinghamshire NG17 2HU Tel. 0800 318686

Books to read
Beliefs and Cultures: Hindu by Anita Ganeri (Franklin Watts, 2004)
Celebrate: Diwali by Mike Hirst (Hodder Wayland, 1999)
Celebration Stories: Coming Home – A Story About Diwali by Kerena Marchant (Hodder Wayland, 2002)
Great Religious Leaders: Krishna and Hinduism by Kerena Marchant (Hodder Wayland, 2002)
Hindu Festivals Cookbook by Kerena Marchant (Hodder Wayland, 2001)
Hindu Festival Tales by Kerena Marchant (Hodder Wayland, 2000)
My Life, My Religion: Hindu Priest by Rasamandala Das (Franklin Watts, 2001)
Storyteller: Hindu Stories by Anita Ganeri (Evans, 2004)
Where we Worship: Hindu Mandir by Angela Wood (Franklin Watts, 1998)
World of Festivals: Divali by Dilip Kadodwala (Evans, 1999)
World of Festivals: Holi by Dilip Kadodwala (Evans, 2000)
World Religions: Hinduism by Catherine Prior (Franklin Watts, 1999)

Photopacks
Hindus photopack, by the Westhill Project, available from Adrian Leech, Westhill RE Centre, Tel. 0121 415 2258. email: a.leech@bham.ac.uk
Living Religions: Hinduism posterpack and booklet (Nelson Thornes)

Websites
www.iskcon.org A comprehensive web page containing prayers and meditations on Krishna, recipes and pages on music, dance and art.
www.hindunet.org Includes a Hindu calendar, glossary of terms and information on Hindu customs, scriptures and worship.
www.theresite.org.uk Includes curriculum resources and IT in RE pages with details of CD-Roms, software and videos, and TV and radio programmes.

Index